COLOR BY INTERVAL
geometric interval designs

by SHARON KAPLAN

Just imagine - *a theory book that is artistic in design!*
The instructions at the bottom of each page
assign a certain color to a specific interval;
the student colors the intervals
and creates an interesting geometric design.
The book is carefully structured so that intervals
are presented in a logical progression
and then thoroughly reinforced.
Musicians of all ages and all instruments
will enjoy this fascinating way to increase
an important skill. Crayons, markers, colored pencils,
water colors - are all effective.
Mix or match, be creative, enjoy!

COLOR BY INTERVAL
geometric interval designs

by SHARON KAPLAN

CONTENTS

Editor: Carole Flatau

COLOR all squares having 2 line notes RED

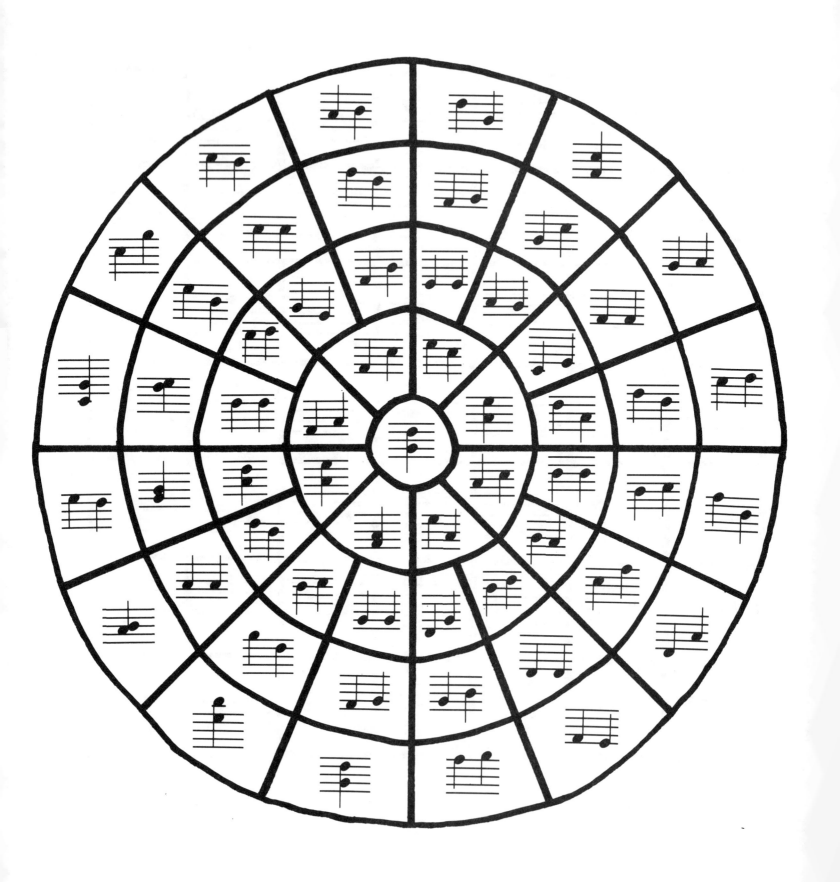

COLOR all shapes having 2 line notes GREEN

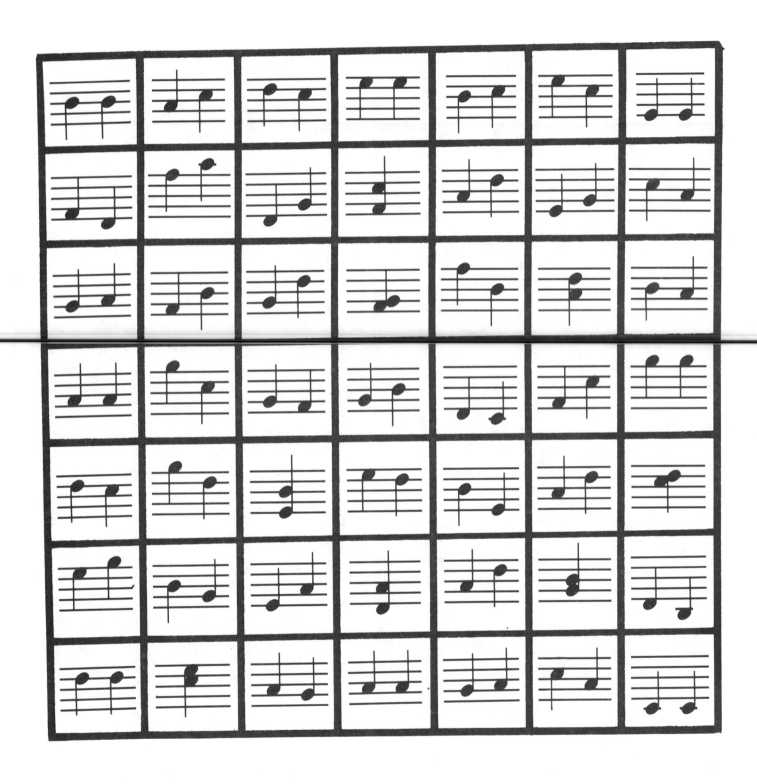

COLOR all squares with two space notes YELLOW

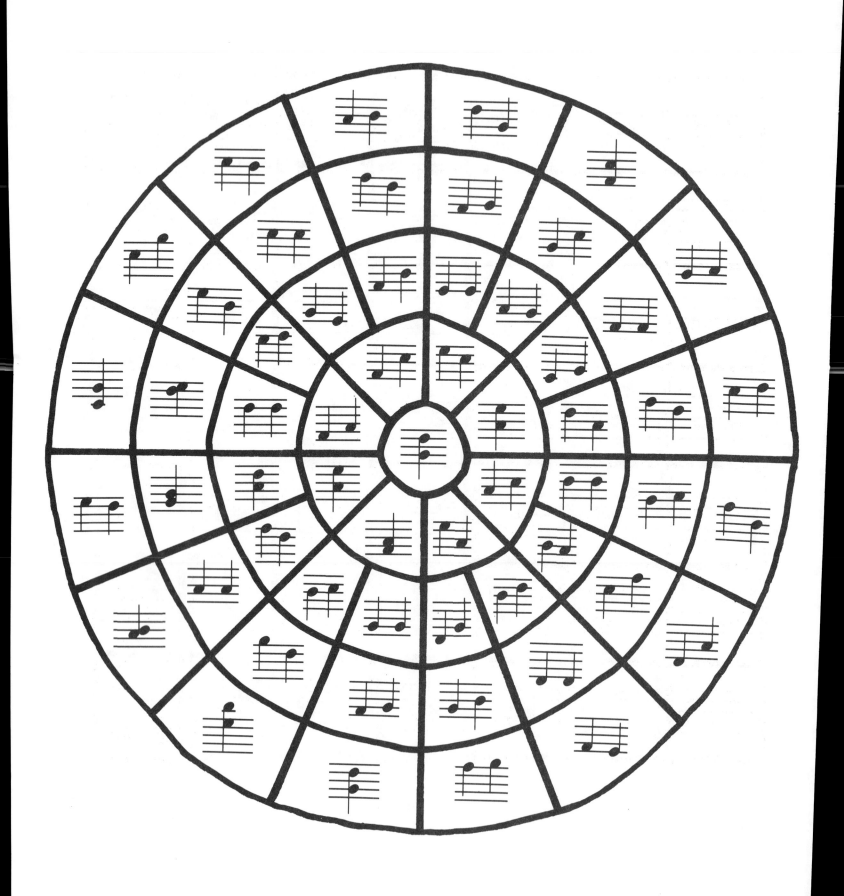

COLOR all shapes with two space notes PURPLE

COLOR all squares with one line note and one space note ORANGE

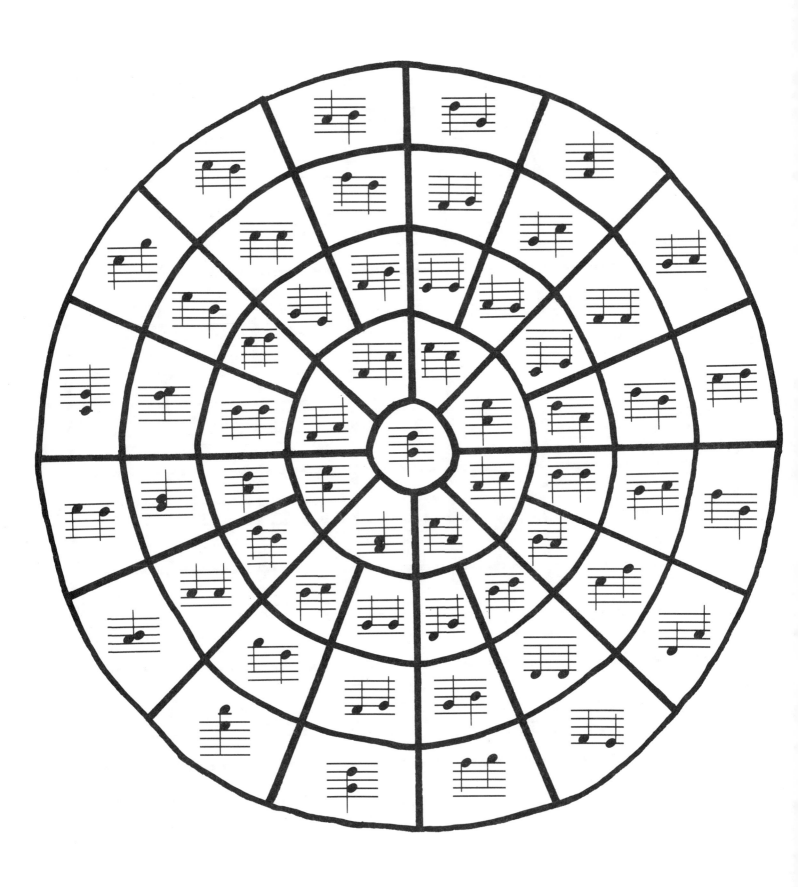

COLOR all shapes with one line note and one space note BLUE

COLOR all repeated notes RED

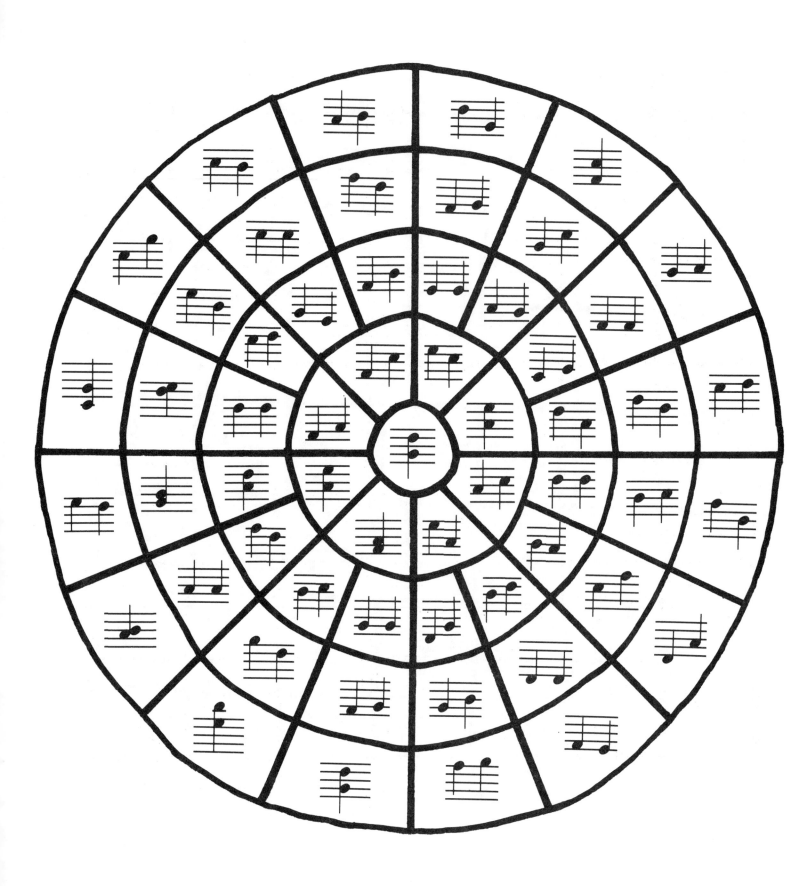

COLOR all repeated notes GREEN

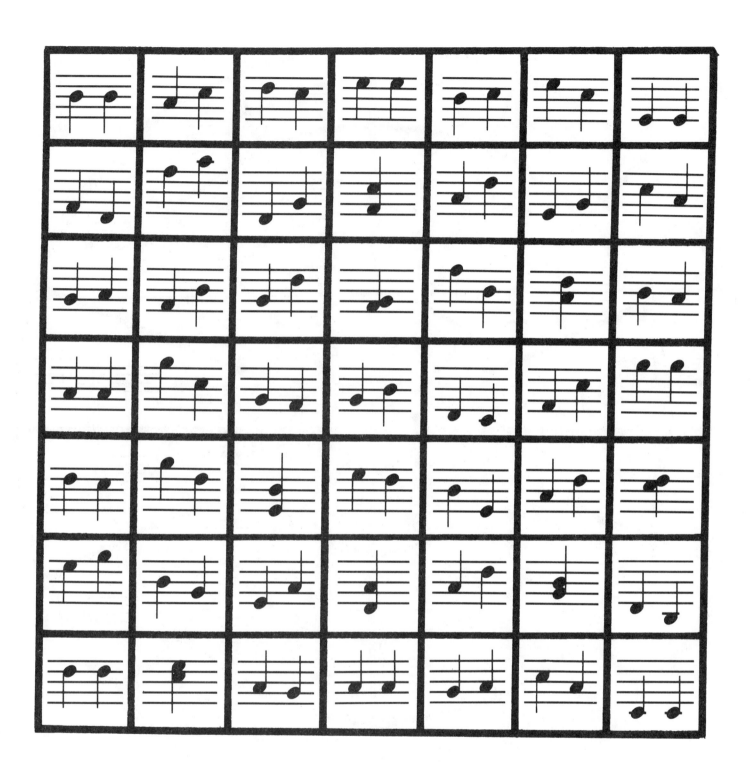

COLOR all 2nds VIOLET

11

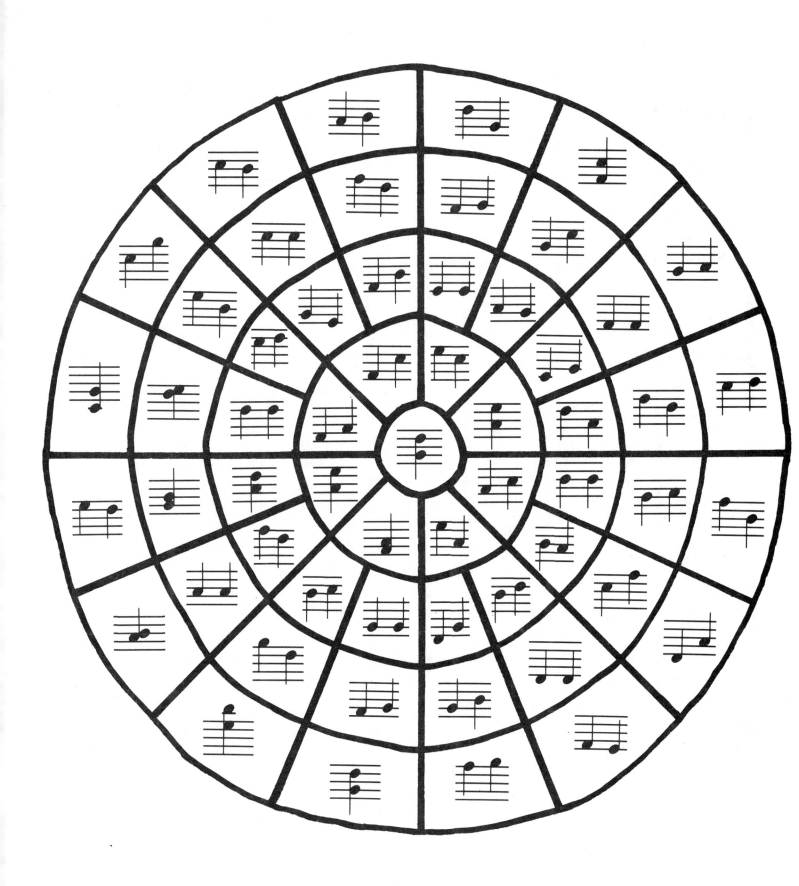

COLOR all 2nds RED

12

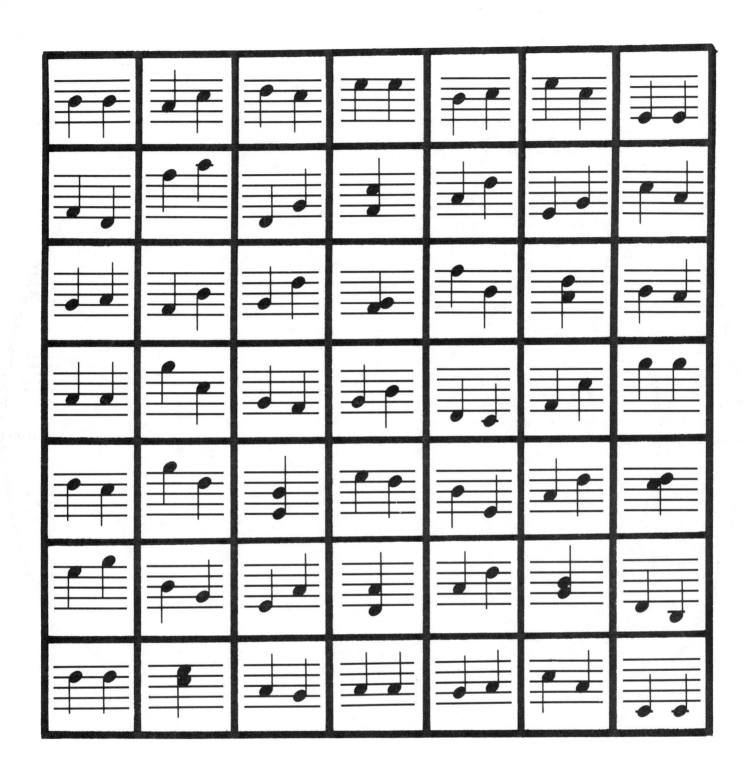

COLOR all 3rds GREEN

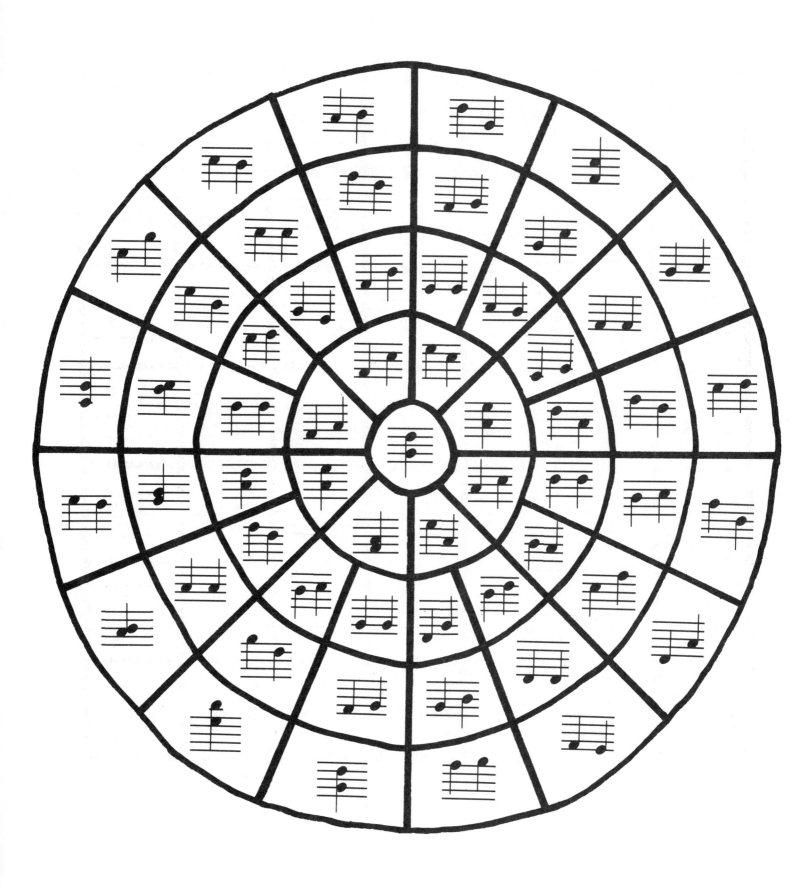

Color all 3rds ORANGE

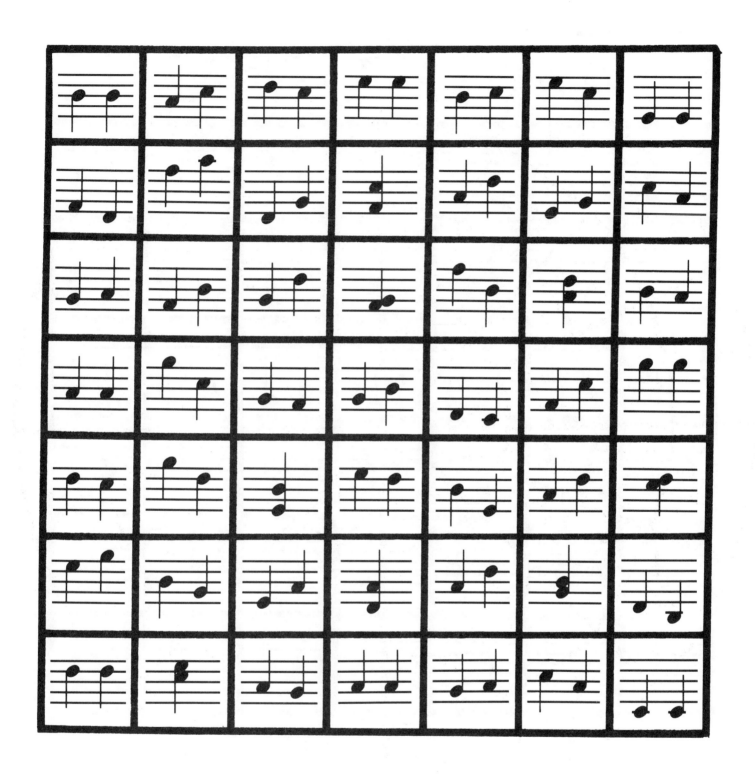

COLOR all 3rds BLUE
then COLOR all remaining squares with two line notes RED

15

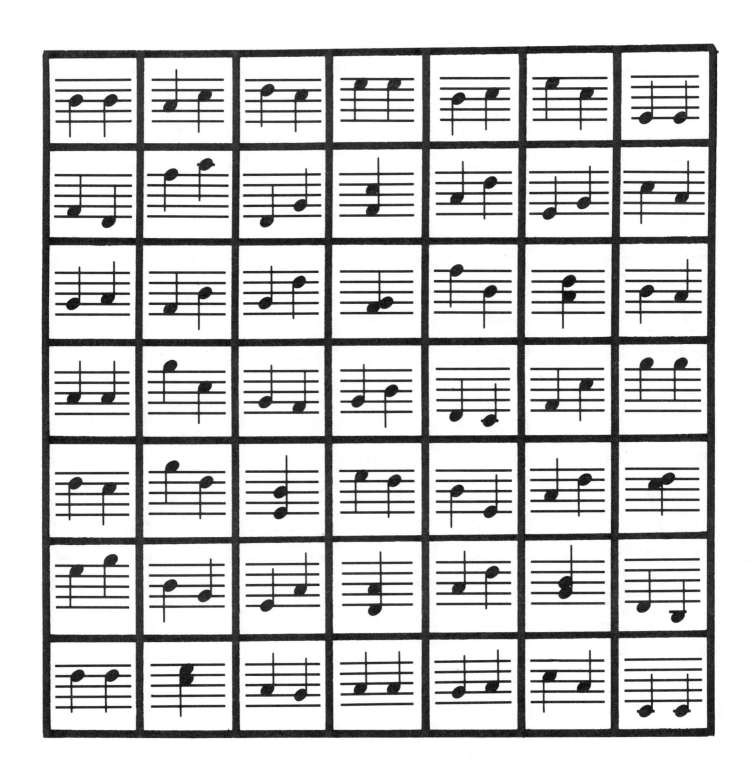

COLOR all squares with two line notes ORANGE
then COLOR all 3rds BROWN

16

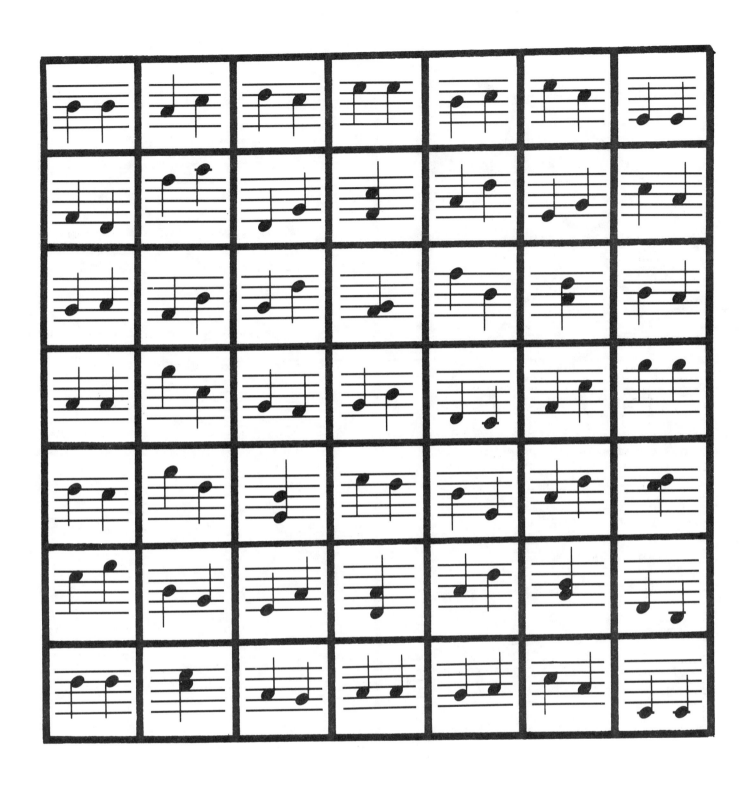

COLOR all 2nds BLUE
COLOR all 3rds GOLD

17

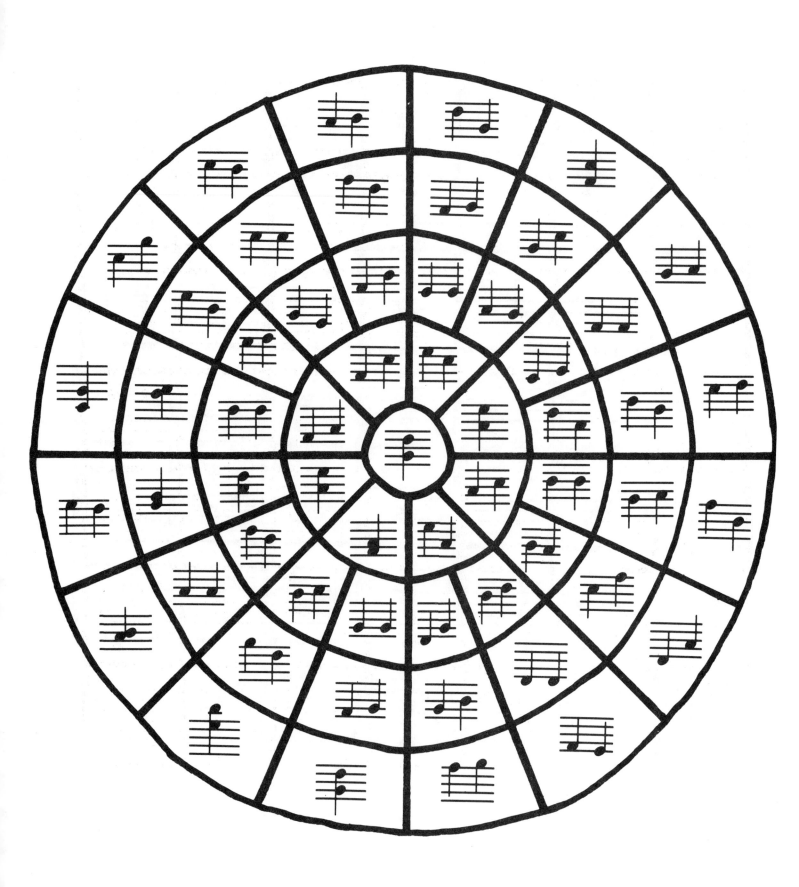

COLOR all 2nds YELLOW
COLOR all 3rds BLUE

18

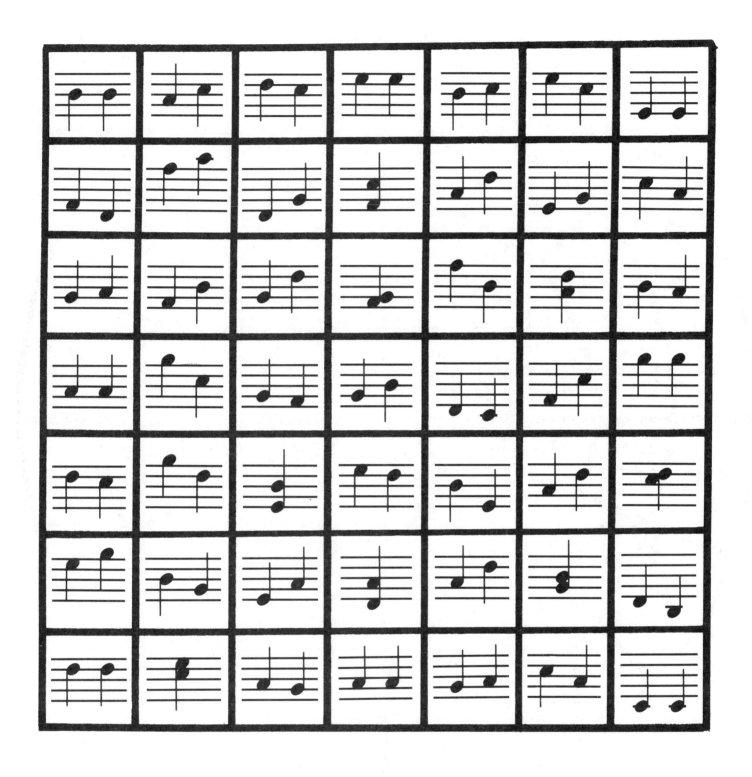

COLOR all 3rds and all repeated notes ORANGE

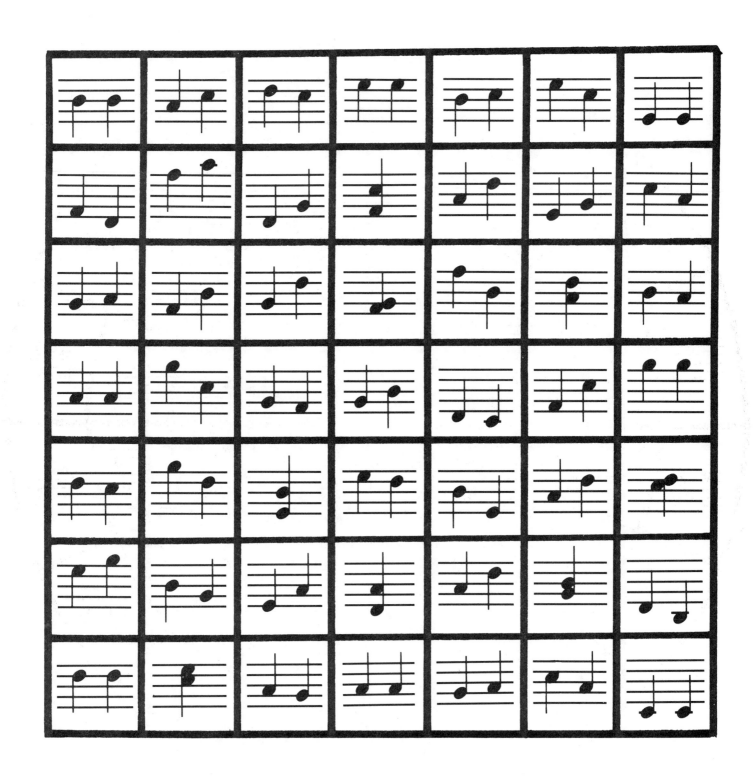

COLOR all 4ths PINK

20

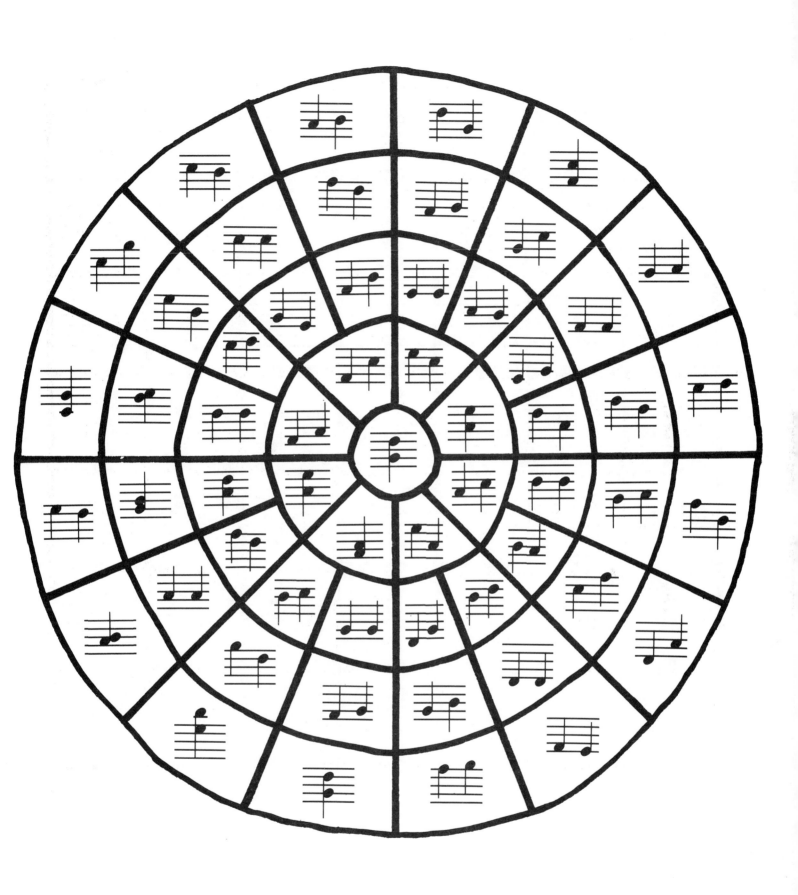

COLOR all 4ths BLUE

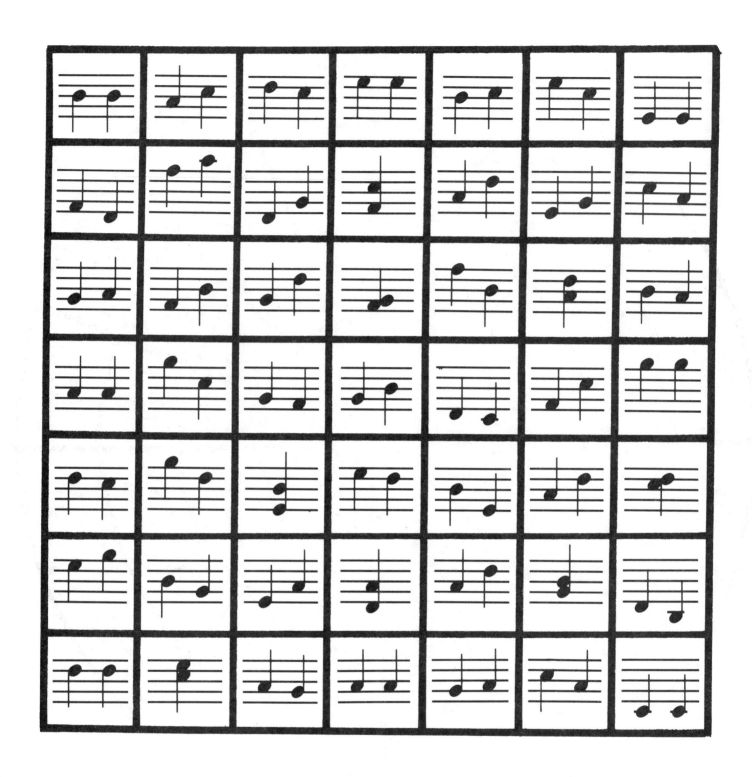

COLOR all squares with two line notes BLUE
COLOR all 4ths ORANGE

22

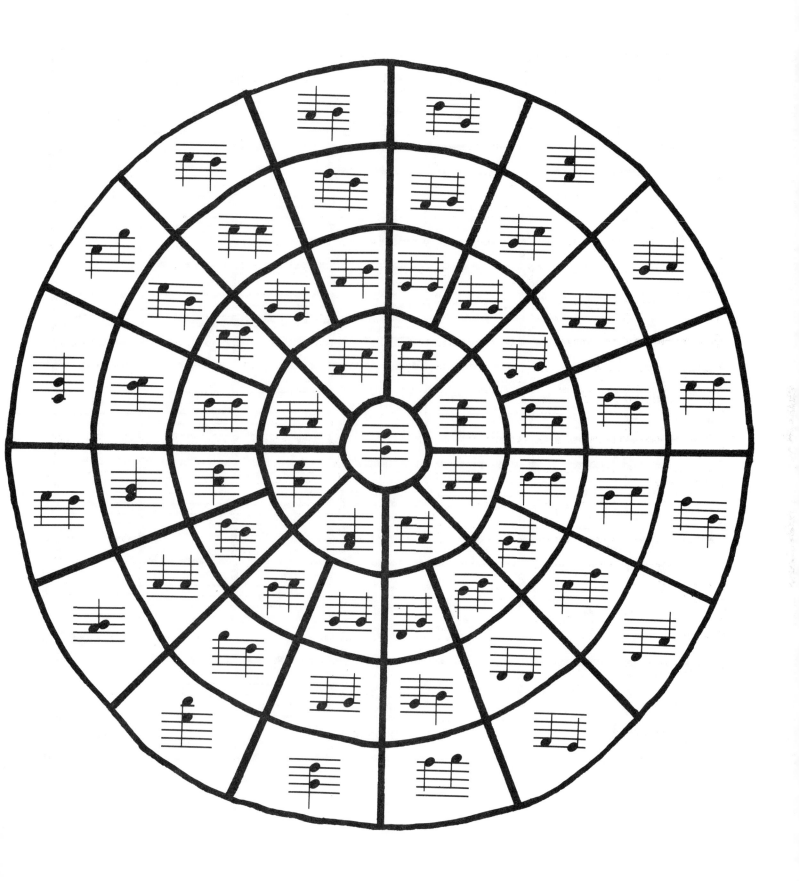

COLOR all 4ths BLUE
COLOR all shapes with two line notes PURPLE
COLOR all shapes with two space notes PURPLE

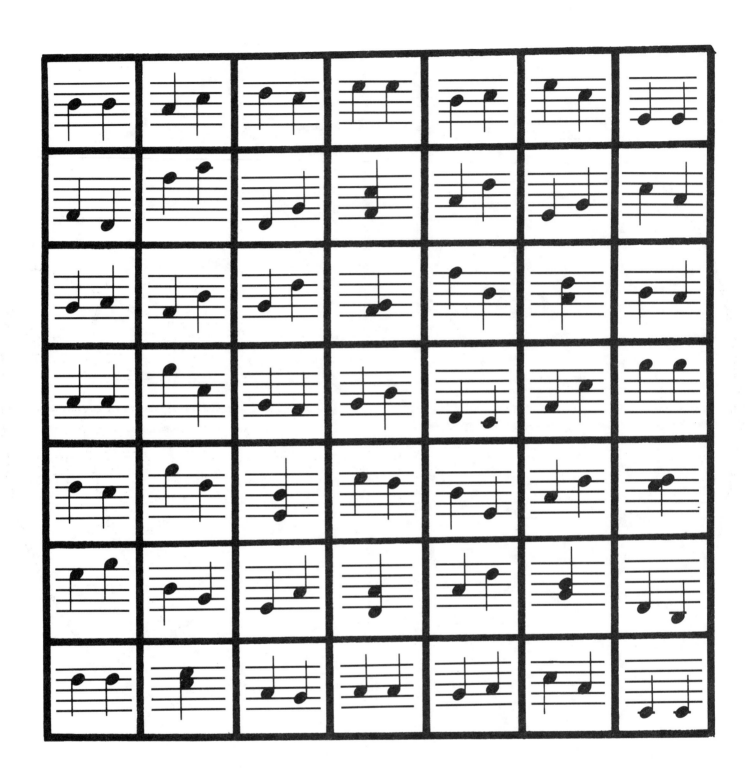

COLOR all 2nds RED
COLOR all 4ths ORANGE

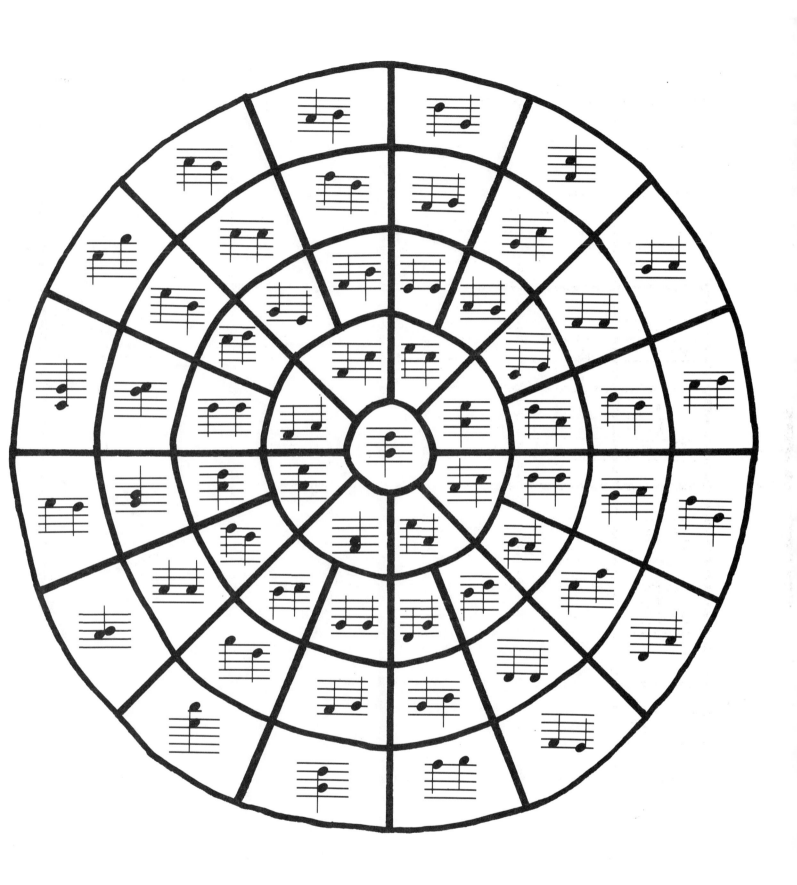

COLOR all 3rds GOLD
COLOR all 4ths BLACK

25

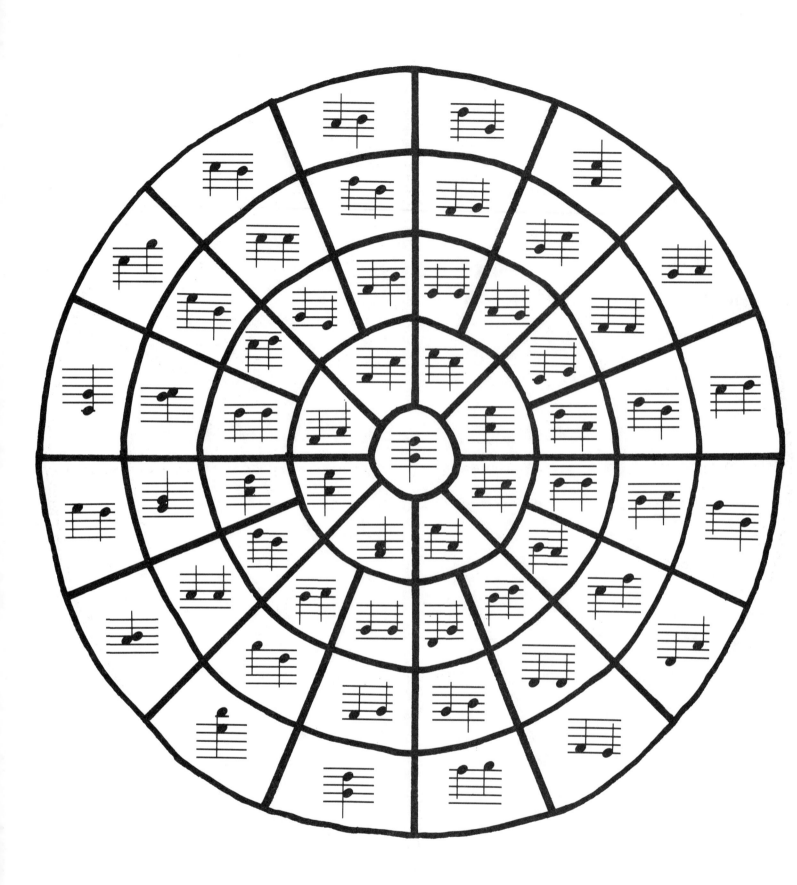

COLOR all 2nds BLUE
COLOR all 4ths GREEN

26

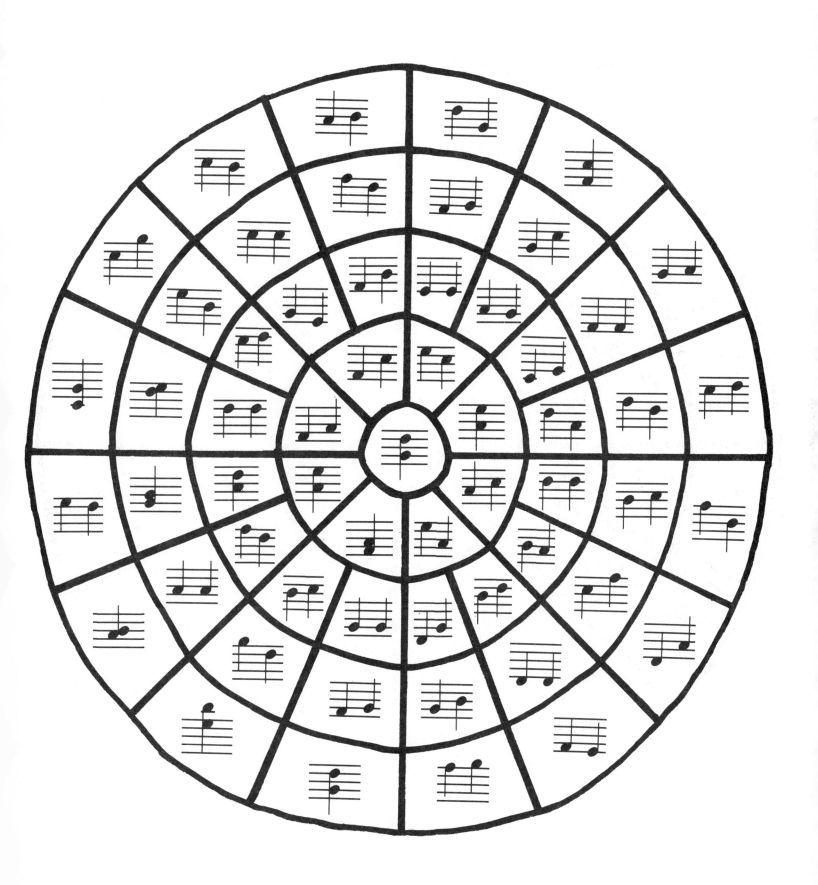

COLOR all 4ths BLUE-GREEN
COLOR all repeated notes BLUE-GREEN

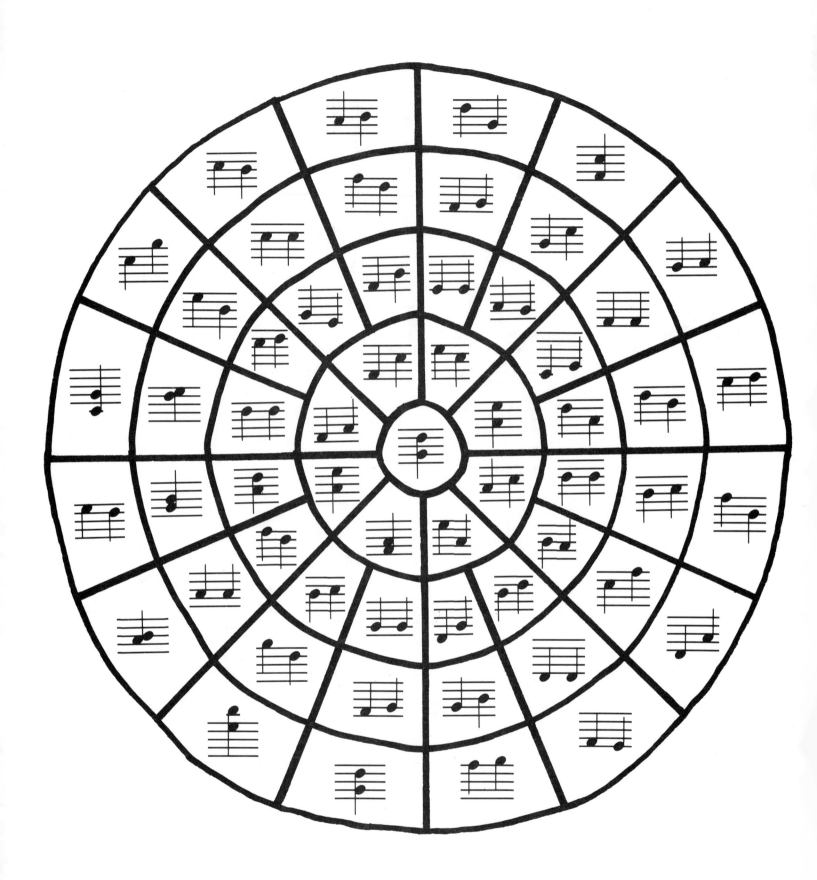

COLOR all repeated notes PURPLE
COLOR all 2nds PURPLE
Color all 4ths YELLOW

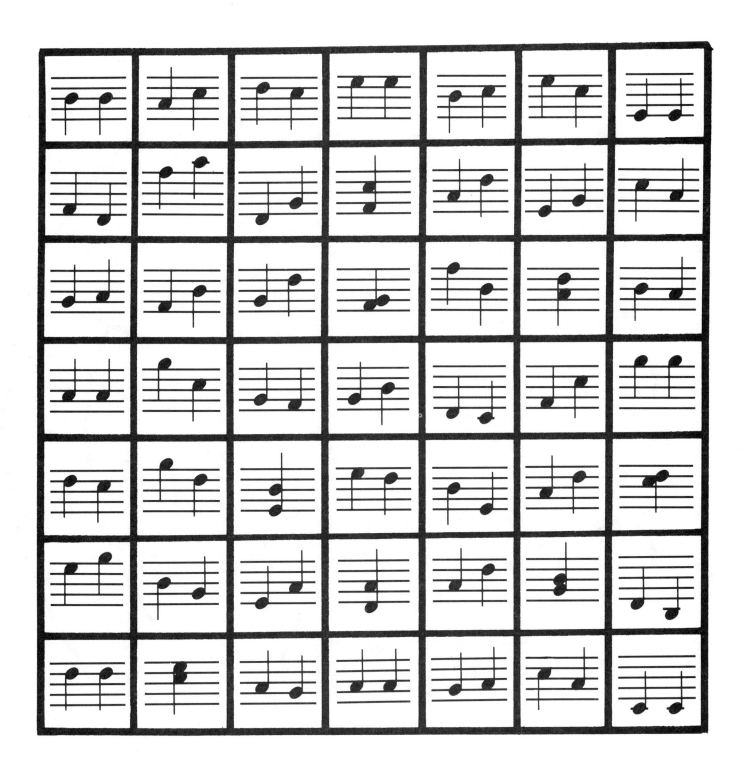

COLOR all 5ths BROWN

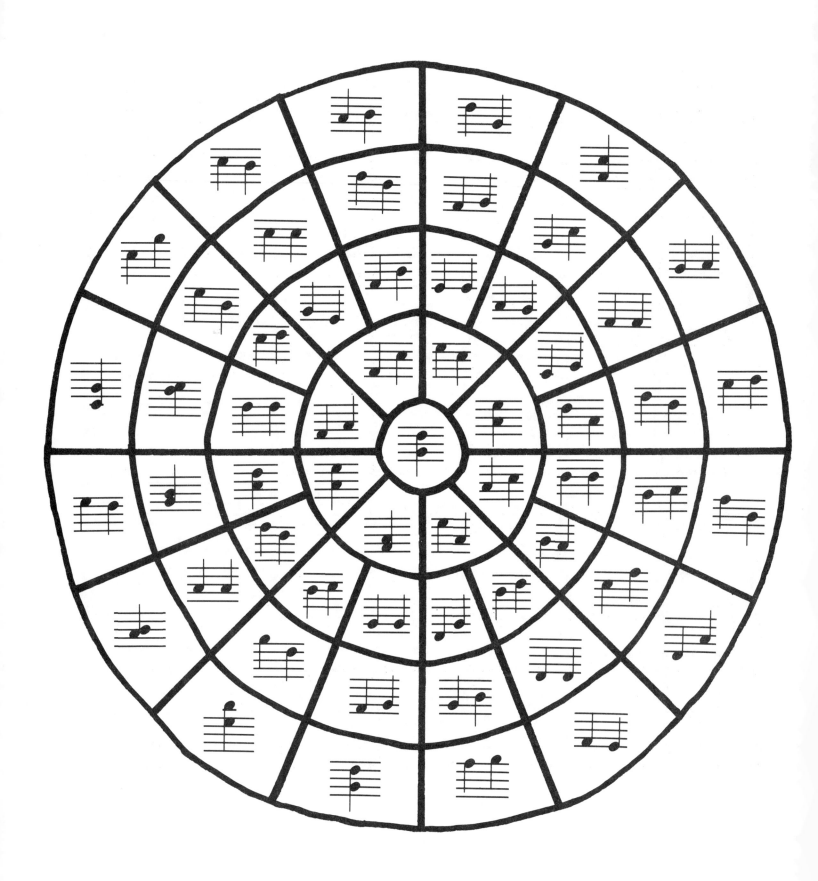

COLOR all 5ths YELLOW

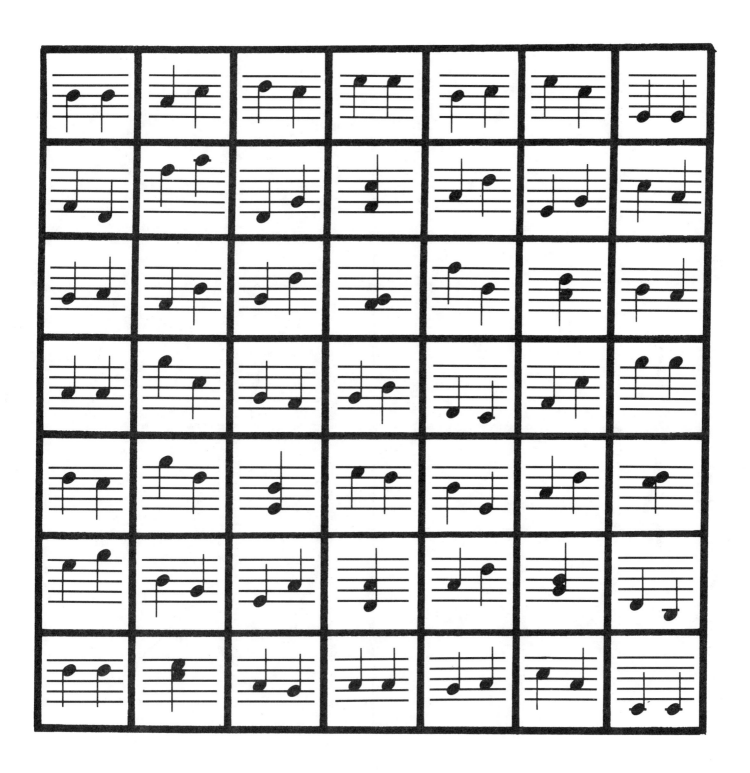

COLOR all 5ths GREEN
COLOR all repeated notes BLUE

31

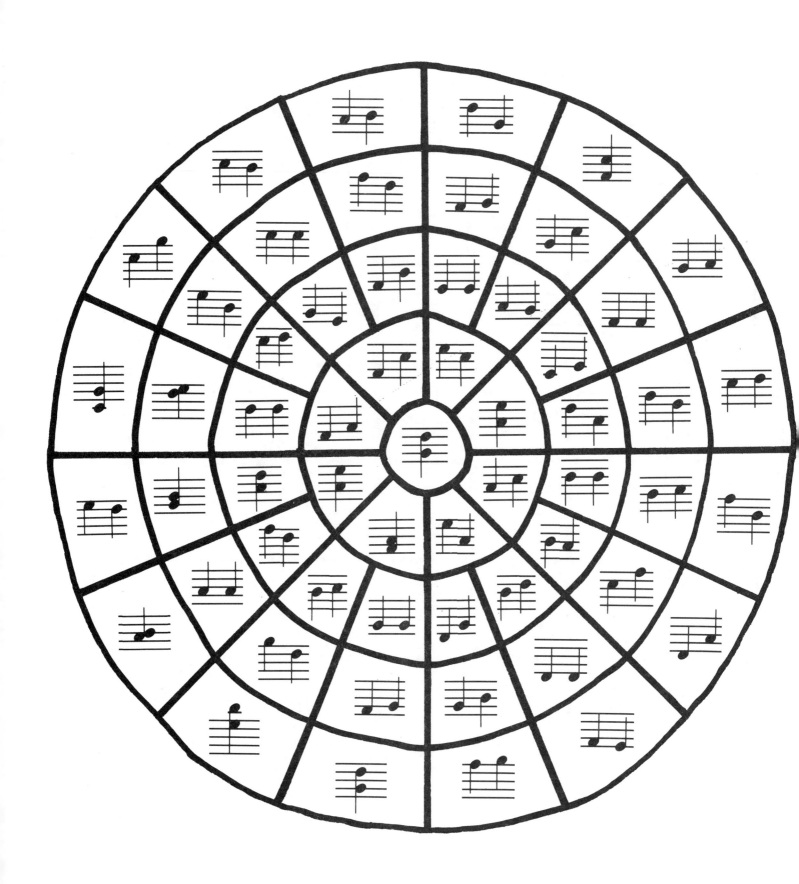

COLOR all 5ths BLACK
then COLOR remaining shapes with two space notes YELLOW

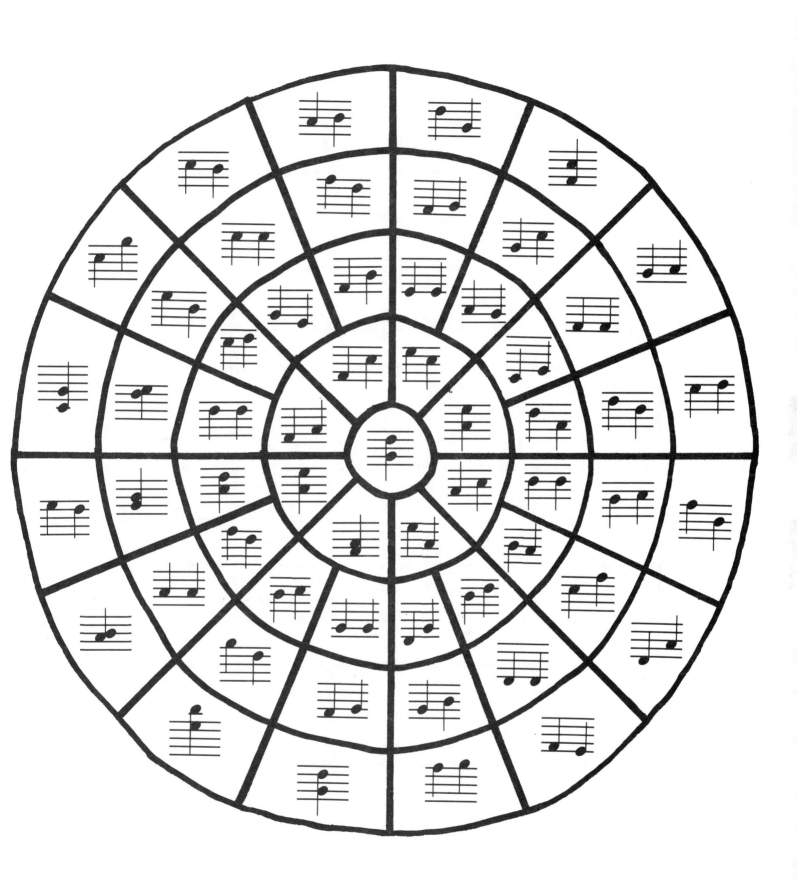

**COLOR all shapes with two space notes YELLOW
then COLOR all 5ths BLACK**

33

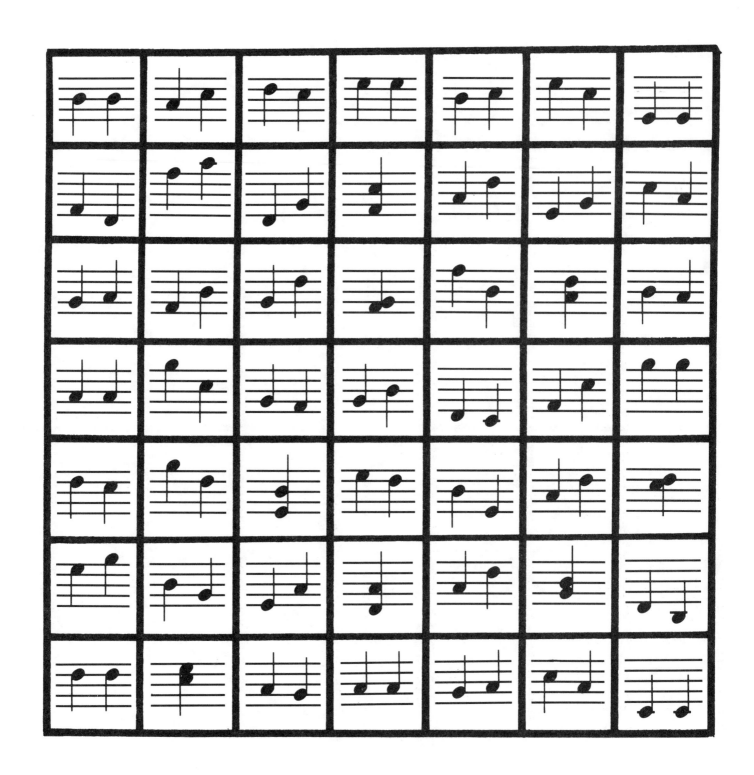

COLOR all 4ths PINK
COLOR all 5ths PURPLE

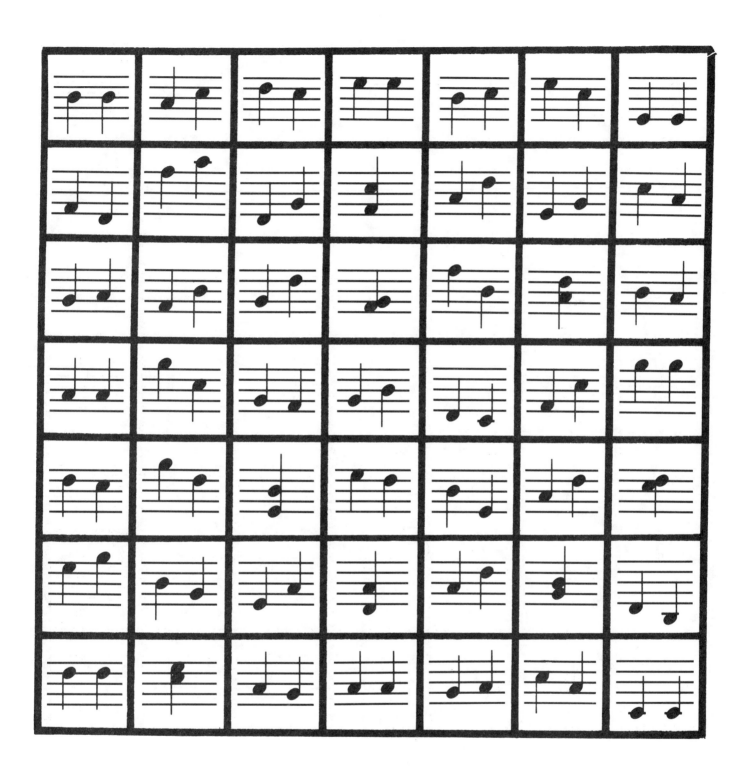

COLOR all 4ths BROWN
COLOR all 2nds BROWN
COLOR all 5ths GOLD
COLOR all 3rds GOLD

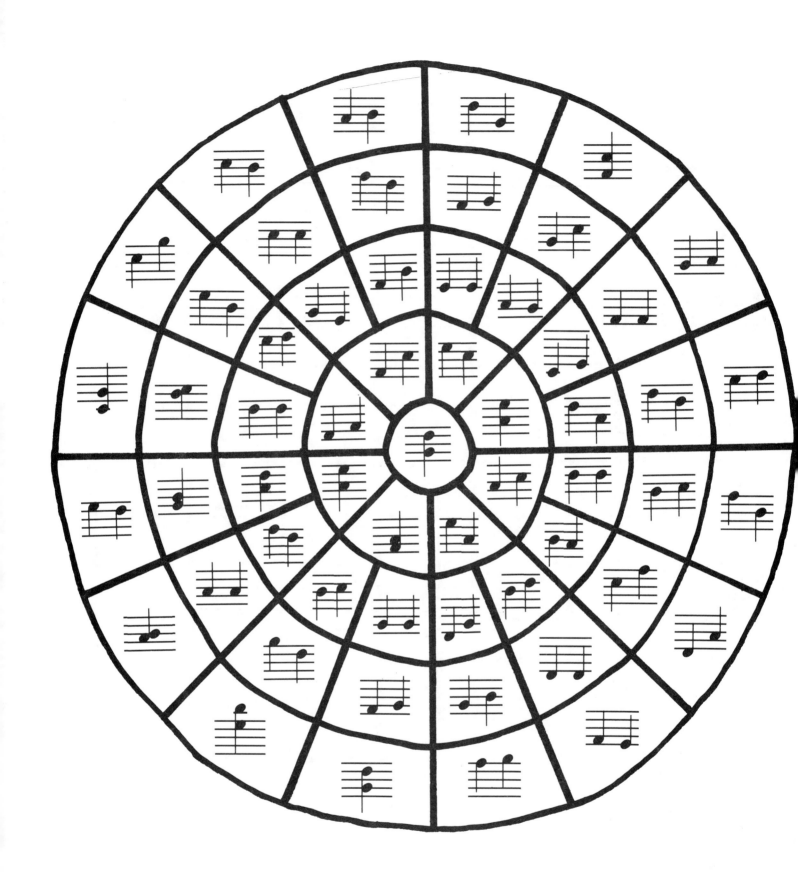

COLOR all 4ths BLUE
COLOR all 5ths YELLOW

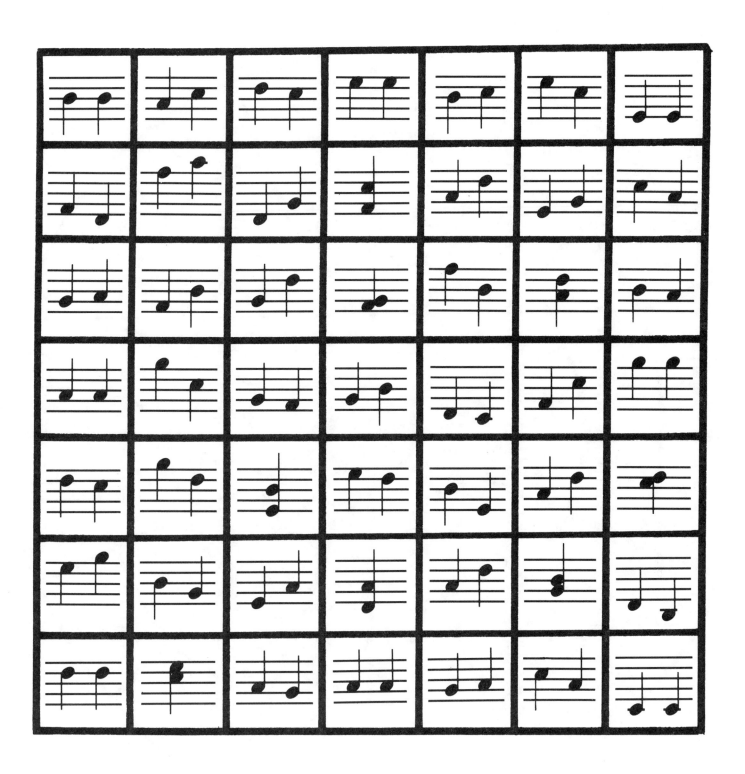

COLOR all 2nds GREEN
COLOR all 5ths ORANGE

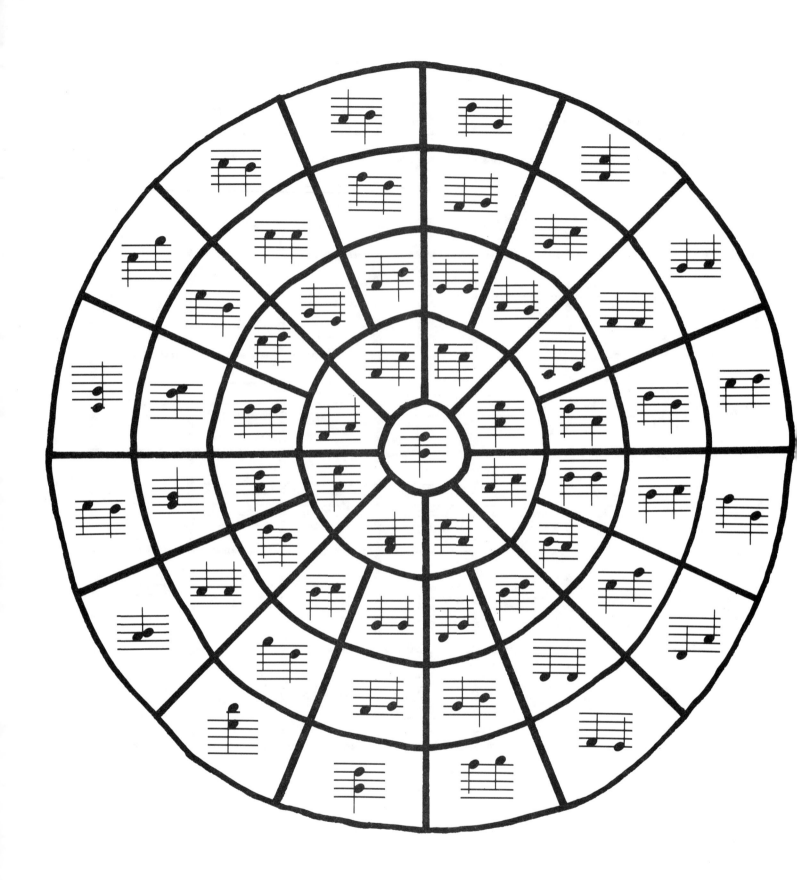

COLOR all 3rds RED
COLOR all 5ths GREEN

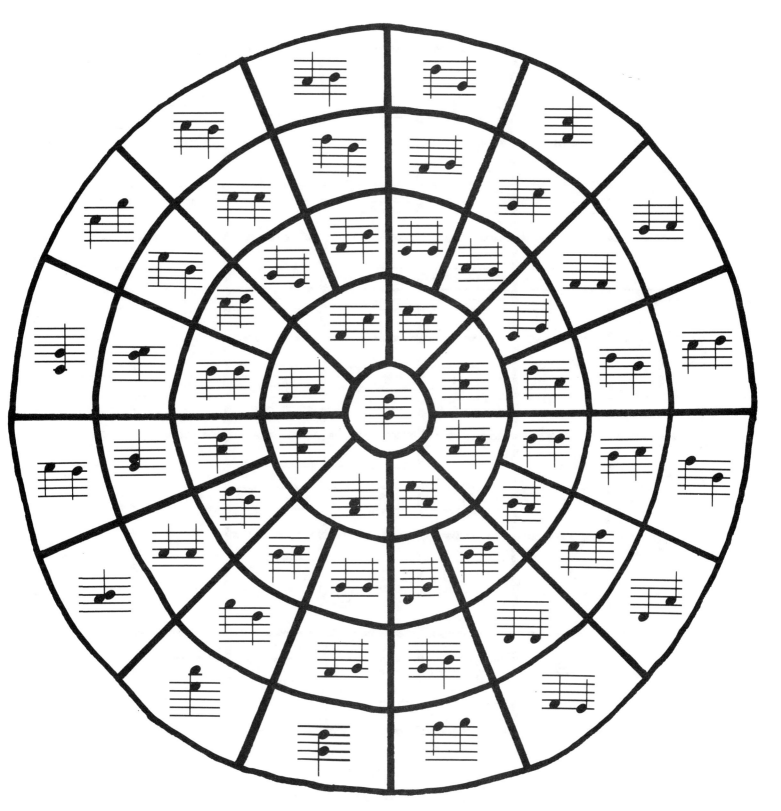

PICK YOUR OWN COLORS

2nds _____
3rds _____
4ths _____
5ths _____
What's left with no color? ___

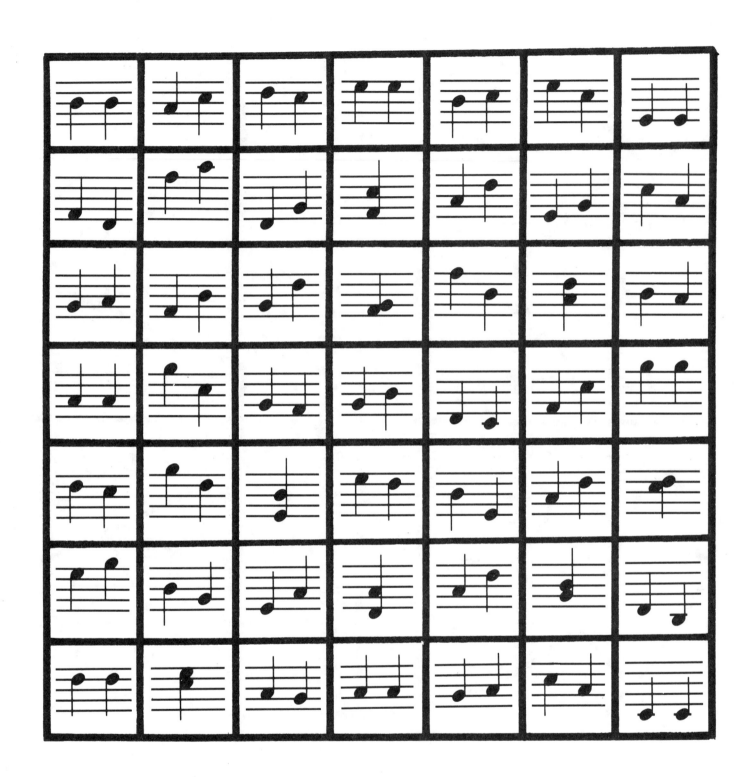

PICK YOUR OWN COLORS

2nds _____

3rds _____

4ths _____

5ths _____

What's left with no color? _____